Driver Ants

Written by Marilyn Woolley

Flying Start
to Literacy®

Contents

What are driver ants?   4

Millions of ants   6

    In a driver ant colony   7

    The largest ants   8

Terrifying hunters   10

A huge army   14

    Blind killers   16

Hunting the hunters   18

    Gorillas   18

    Chimpanzees   21

Helping out   22

Glossary   24

What are driver ants?

Driver ants are the largest ants in the world. They are also called killer ants.

Driver ants kill all living things that they find as they march across the forest floor and through the grasslands looking for food. They kill more animals than any other animal in their habitat.

Millions of driver ants go hunting together. They terrify all animals. Animals run to escape when they hear the driver ants coming.

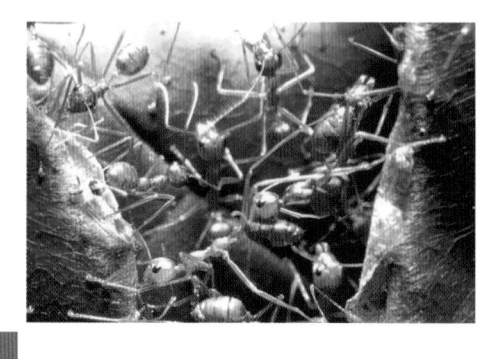

FACT

Driver ants live in rainforests and grasslands in parts of Africa.

Millions of ants

Driver ants live together in colonies in huge nests under the ground. Driver ants have the largest colonies of any ants. Up to 20 million driver ants or more live in the one colony.

In a driver ant colony

There are four types of driver ants in a colony. Each type of ant does a different job.

Queen ant
The queen ant lays one to two million eggs each month.

Worker ants
Worker ants find food for the queen and look after the eggs.

Soldier ants
Soldier ants guard the nest and protect the queen and worker ants.

Male ants
Male ants leave the nest when they hatch. They live alone and return to the colony during the mating season to mate with the queen.

soldier ant

The largest ants

The queen ant is the largest ant in the world. It can grow up to five centimetres long.

But not all driver ants are this big. Worker ants are only half a centimetre long.

Soldier ants are about 1.5 centimetres long.

Male driver ants grow up to three centimetres long. They have wings.

worker ant

HOW BIG ARE THEY?

queen ant: 5 centimetres

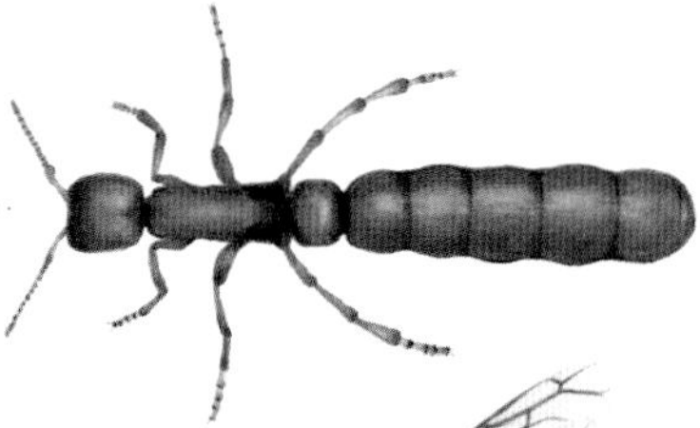

male ant: 3 centimetres

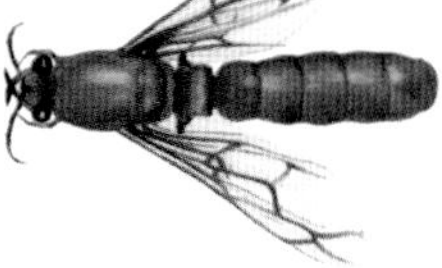

soldier ant: 1.5 centimetres

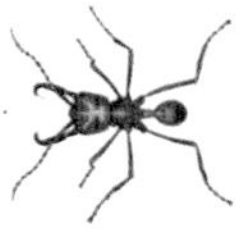

worker ant: 0.5 centimetres

Terrifying hunters

Driver ants eat insects, spiders, earthworms and any other animals, including mammals and reptiles.

Each day, millions of ants leave the nest to hunt for food. As they march out of the nest, they make a loud, terrifying rumble.

When the other animals in the jungle hear this noise they run away to escape the ants.

The ants eat young or injured birds, reptiles, or mammals left behind in the rush and panic. If an animal is caught by these ants, it will not survive.

Driver ants don't use a sting to attack animals. They have large powerful jaws that they use to stab and tear animals apart.

Driver ants work together to attack animals that are much bigger than themselves. They use their sharp jaws to cut up the animal and carry it back to their nest for food.

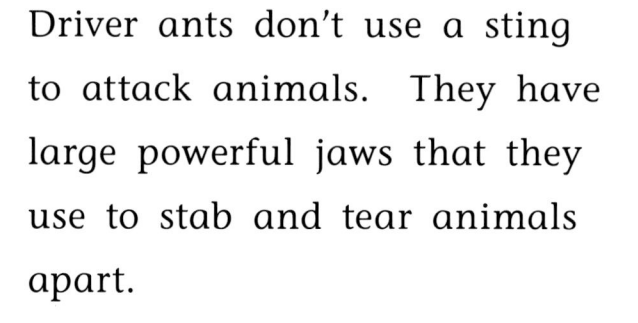

Driver ants eat so much food that they eat all the animals in the area. They stay in each nest for only three or four weeks, then they move to a new place that has lots of animals to eat.

Driver ants have strong, powerful jaws.

A huge army

When driver ants hunt for food or move their nest, they move together as a huge army, twenty-five metres wide and five metres deep. This is called swarming.

The soldier ants stay on each side of this swarming army. They protect other driver ants by keeping their two strong jaws open, ready to bite and tear off pieces of flesh of any animal near them.

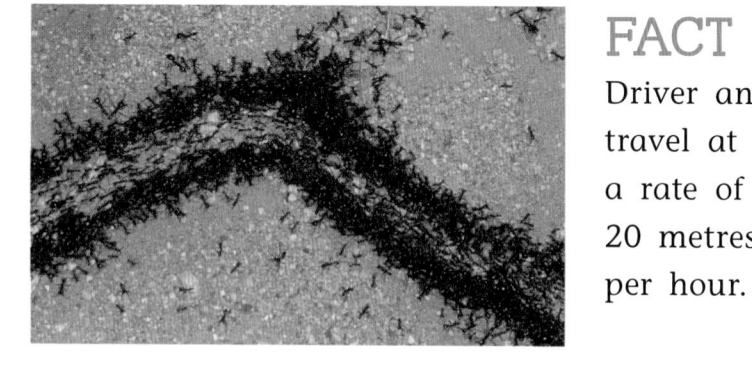

FACT

Driver ants travel at a rate of 20 metres per hour.

Blind killers

Driver ants do not have eyes so they cannot see, but they can still find their way around. They use touch, smell and chemical signals to find food and to communicate with each other.

Driver ants cannot swim, but they can cross water. To do this, they build a bridge using leaves and their own bodies. It is sometimes called a living bridge.

Hunting the hunters

Two animals have worked out ways to gather up and eat driver ants from underground nests.

Gorillas

Gorillas attack the underground nests of driver ants so they can eat the ants.

Gorillas have strong powerful hands. A gorilla reaches into the nest with one of its hands and scrunches up the ants so they cannot bite. Then the gorilla moves the ants quickly into its mouth so they cannot get away.

Chimpanzees

Chimpanzees make two different tools to gather the driver ants from their nests.

First a chimpanzee uses a thick branch to punch or dig a hole in the ants' nest. Then the chimpanzee puts a thin stem of a plant or a stiff blade of grass into this hole and wobbles it from side to side.

Some ants come out to protect their nest from an attack and climb up this thin stem. But as the ants climb higher, the stick bends under them and they cannot swarm together to fight back.

Then the chimpanzee runs its hand along the stem, pulls the ants off and eats them in one big mouthful.

Helping out

Driver ants are dangerous because they swarm in such large numbers and they will attack and eat any living thing. But this is not always a bad thing.

Driver ants eat the bugs and other pests that destroy farm crops. When they swarm into people's houses, they eat all the bugs and pests.

Driver ants can be helpful as well as dangerous.